FARM ANIMALS
Sheep

by Emily K. Green

BELLWETHER MEDIA • MINNEAPOLIS, MN

Note to Librarians, Teachers, and Parents:

Blastoff! Readers are carefully developed by literacy experts and combine standards-based content with developmentally appropriate text.

Level 1 provides the most support through repetition of high-frequency words, light text, predictable sentence patterns, and strong visual support.

Level 2 offers early readers a bit more challenge through varied simple sentences, increased text load, and less repetition of high-frequency words.

Level 3 advances early-fluent readers toward fluency through increased text and concept load, less reliance on visuals, longer sentences, and more literary language.

Whichever book is right for your reader, Blastoff! Readers are the perfect books to build confidence and encourage a love of reading that will last a lifetime!

This edition first published in 2007 by Bellwether Media.

No part of this publication may be reproduced in whole or in part without written permission of the publisher. For information regarding permission, write to Bellwether Media Inc., Attention: Permissions Department, Post Office Box 1C, Minnetonka, MN 55345-9998.

Library of Congress Cataloging-in-Publication Data
Green, Emily K., 1966–
  Sheep / by Emily K. Green.
    p. cm. — (Blastoff! readers. Farm animals)
Summary: "A basic introduction to sheep and how they live on the farm. Simple text and full color photographs. Developed by literacy experts for students in kindergarten through third grade"—Provided by publisher.
  Includes bibliographical references and index.
  ISBN-13: 978-1-60014-069-3 (hardcover : alk. paper)
  ISBN-10: 1-60014-069-6 (hardcover : alk. paper)
  1. Sheep—Juvenile literature. I. Title.

SF375.2.G74 2007
636.3–dc22   2006035309

Contents

Many farms
have sheep.

Sheep stay in a group called a **flock**.

A female sheep is a **ewe**. A baby sheep is a **lamb**.

A male sheep is a **ram**. Both male and female sheep may have horns.

Sheep eat fresh grass or **hay**.

13

Sheep have four hard feet called **hoofs**. Sheep have two toes on each hoof.

hoof

Sheep have thick hair called **wool**. Wool keeps sheep warm on cold days.

Farmers **shear** the wool from their sheep in spring.

People make
sweaters and other
warm clothes from
wool. Wool keeps
you warm!

Glossary

ewe—a female sheep

flock—a group of animals that stays together

hay—grass or other plants that are cut, dried, and fed to animals

hoofs—the hard feet of sheep

lamb—a baby sheep

ram—a male sheep

shear—to cut off the hair of a sheep

wool—the thick, curly hair of a sheep

To Learn More

AT THE LIBRARY

Parker, Mary Jessie. *Wild and Woolly*. New York: Dutton, 2005.

Scotton, Rob. *Russell the Sheep*. New York: HarperCollins, 2005.

Stohner, Anu. *Brave Charlotte*. New York: Bloomsbury Children's Books, 2005.

ON THE WEB

Learning more about farm animals is as easy as 1, 2, 3.

1. Go to www.factsurfer.com

2. Enter "farm animals" into search box.

3. Click the "Surf" button and you will see a list of related web sites.

With factsurfer.com, finding more information is just a click away.

Index

The photographs in this book are reproduced through the courtesy of: Eric Gevaert, front cover; Anna Dzondzua, p. 5; Lindsay McWilliams, p. 7; Eshter Groen, p. 9; Bruce, p. 11; Dragan Trifunovic, p. 13; Laryssa Dodz, p. 15; Eric Gevaert, p. 17; SuperStock/age fotostock, p. 19; Nancy Brown/Alamy, p. 21.

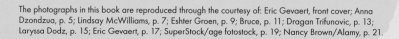